It's a

Sharon Dalgleish

Lexile® measure: 760L
For more information visit: www.Lexile.com

Brainwaves Orange
It's a Mystery
ISBN 978 1 86509 484 7

Copyright © 2003 Blake Publishing
Reprinted 2006, 2010, 2014
Lexile Copyright © 2013 MetaMetrics, Inc.

Published by Blake Education Pty Ltd
ABN 074 266 023
Locked Bag 2022
Glebe NSW 2037
Ph: (02) 8585 4085
Fax: (02) 8585 4058
Email: info@blake.com.au
Website: www.blake.com.au

Series publisher: Sharon Dalgleish
Designer: Cliff Watt
Photo research: Annette Crueger

Picture credits: pg 14, 16 and 18-19
photolibrary.com; pg 23-27 and 29 AUSTRAL

Printed by Thumbprints UTD

Contents

Enter the World of the Unexplained

In 1872, a ship called the *Mary Celeste* was found drifting in the North Atlantic Ocean—with no-one on board.

The crew of the *Mary Celeste* had disappeared! Some people thought that the ship was attacked by a giant octopus. Or that the crew drowned when an island rose from the sea and then sank again. Or that a whirlwind sucked the crew off the decks. Or that everyone fell overboard into the mouths of hungry sharks.

The Mystery of the Ship that Sailed Herself

Ten people had set sail on the *Mary Celeste*: the captain, his wife and young daughter and seven crewmen. They were never seen again—and the mystery of what happened to them has never been solved.

The official explanation of the *Mary Celeste* mystery was that the crew murdered the captain and his family, and then escaped onto another ship. But if this theory is correct, why was there no sign of a struggle on the ship? And why were the valuables still on board? Read the case notes on the next page. What do you think happened?

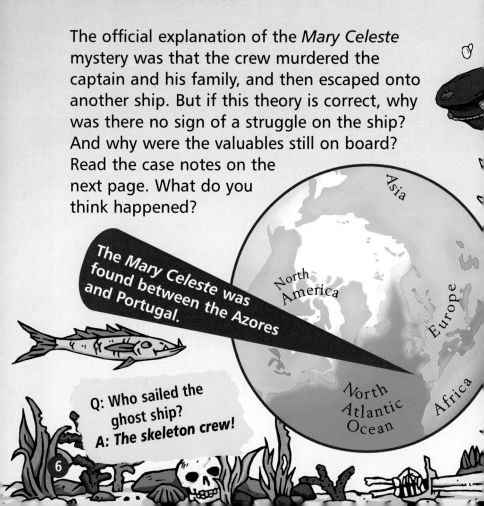

The *Mary Celeste* was found between the Azores and Portugal.

Asia

North America

Europe

North Atlantic Ocean

Africa

Q: Who sailed the ghost ship?
A: The skeleton crew!

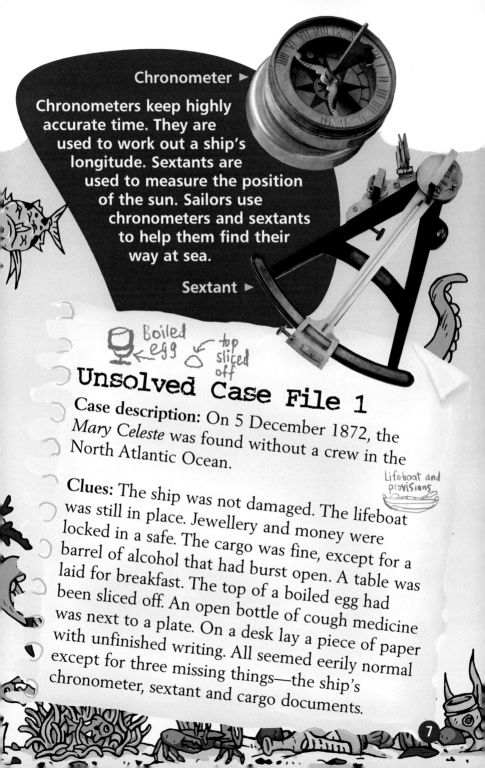

Chronometer ▶

Chronometers keep highly accurate time. They are used to work out a ship's longitude. Sextants are used to measure the position of the sun. Sailors use chronometers and sextants to help them find their way at sea.

Sextant ▶

Boiled egg ← top sliced off

Unsolved Case File 1

Case description: On 5 December 1872, the *Mary Celeste* was found without a crew in the North Atlantic Ocean.

Lifeboat and provisions

Clues: The ship was not damaged. The lifeboat was still in place. Jewellery and money were locked in a safe. The cargo was fine, except for a barrel of alcohol that had burst open. A table was laid for breakfast. The top of a boiled egg had been sliced off. An open bottle of cough medicine was next to a plate. On a desk lay a piece of paper with unfinished writing. All seemed eerily normal except for three missing things—the ship's chronometer, sextant and cargo documents.

Secrets in Stone

Stonehenge is a group of huge stones in England. It was probably built about 5 000 years ago. So how did its makers manage to transport, shape, raise and connect the giant stones? Even more mysterious, how did they know how to position the stones in exactly the right spots to measure the movements of the sun and moon? The answer is: no-one knows.

There are megaliths, or big stones, all over the world. On Easter Island there are about 900 giant stone heads. The statues are from 3 to 12 metres high. Some weigh over

Stonehenge
The stones are arranged in a series of three rings with an altar stone in the middle. The stones in the outside ring stand about 4.1 m high.

Easter Island is now a national park, watched over by the stern-looking stone heads.

45 tonnes. That's more than the weight of seven elephants! How did the statues get on Easter Island? A **legend** says they walked there. The mystery is still waiting to be solved.

Unsolved Case File 2

Case description: A legend says Stonehenge was built by giants. It was once called the Giants' Dance. In the legend, mysterious giants lifted the huge stones. But why?

Mother Ship

alien pod ships

Landing lights

Theories to investigate:
- It was a great stone-age computer.
- It was a temple to worship the sun.
- It was built by aliens as a landing area for their spaceships.

Beware the Bermuda Triangle!

For centuries, people have reported strange things happening in a triangle-shaped area of the Atlantic Ocean. As Christopher Columbus's ships sailed through in 1492, his compass went haywire. The crew saw great flames of fire crashing into the ocean.

But the area really became famous in 1945. One sunny afternoon, five bomber planes, with 14 men on board, took off into the clear sky. The flight leader radioed that something was wrong with his compass. Then the planes vanished without trace. And so did the rescue plane sent to search for them! Nothing was ever found. No oil slick, no floating wreckage, no bodies. Nothing . . .

Bermuda Triangle Timeline

Vanishing ships. Vanishing aeroplanes. These mysterious vanishing acts—and many, many more—have never been explained.

The *Atlanta*, a British ship, vanishes with 290 people on board.

A British passenger plane disappears with 2 people on board.

1880

1945

194

Flight 19 (five torpedo bomber planes, and their crews) disappears.

Unsolved Case File 3

Case description: If you don't want to vanish, don't fly a plane or sail a ship in the area known as the Bermuda Triangle!

Need to buy!
- One pair of flippers
- One snorkel

Theories to investigate:

- A deadly laser beam pointing up from the bottom of the ocean destroys passing boats and planes.
- Giant sea monsters pull boats under the water.
- Ships and planes are hit by falling **meteors**.
- The magnetic field in the area makes compasses go haywire so that craft become lost.

The Bermuda Triangle's exact location is not clear. Many believe that it covers the area shown below.

The ship *Marine Sulphur Queen* disappears with 39 people on board.

The ship *Marques* disappears with 18 people on board.

1954   1963   1967   1984

A US Navy plane vanishes with 42 people on board.

A cargo plane lost with 4 people on board.

Send It to Forensics

A villain runs from the scene of a crime. He gets away — or so he thinks.

Criminals always take something away from the scene of the crime. It might be the dirt on their shoes. Or it could be a victim's hair on their clothes.

Criminals almost always leave something behind at the scene, too. It might be just a scrap of fabric, a strand of hair, or even a drop of sweat. But these can all be used as **evidence**.

Science on the Case

The best way to catch criminals is to catch them 'red-handed' in the act of committing the crime. Of course, in most cases that is not what happens. Instead, teams of **forensic** scientists use science to solve crimes. They can often point the finger at a **suspect**—and prove he or she did it!

> I knew something w̲ bugging me.

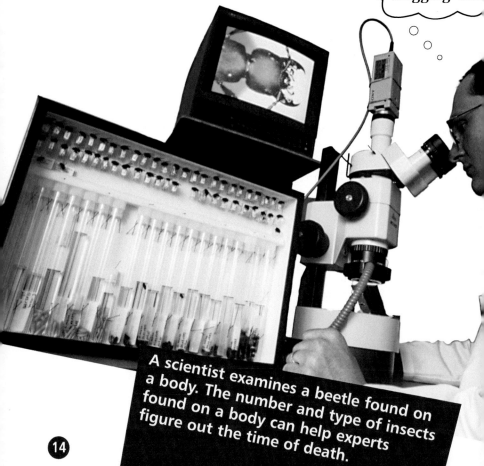

A scientist examines a beetle found on a body. The number and type of insects found on a body can help experts figure out the time of death.

At the scene of a crime, police detectives take detailed notes and photographs, interview **witnesses** and look for clues. They also organise the team of forensic scientists. But the forensic scientists don't just look for evidence that will support the detective's theory. It is their job to uncover all the facts, even if it proves a suspect didn't do it.

Each member of the forensic team has his or her own job.

Crime scene investigators (or CSIs) examine the scene of the crime and collect evidence.

Lab-based forensic scientists carefully analyse all this material, often using the latest technology.

Medical forensic scientists, such as **pathologists** and dentists, are called in if they are needed.

The Scene of the Crime

Have you ever seen a detective in a TV show pick up a clue and hold it in a handkerchief? Or pick up a gun by sticking a pencil through the trigger? This doesn't happen in real life! Crime scene investigators are careful not to leave pieces of themselves—or their pencils or handkerchiefs—on valuable evidence.

Each piece of evidence is sealed in a separate **sterile** plastic bag. The bags are numbered and each person who handles a bag must sign for it. This is called the 'chain of evidence'. If evidence is left unguarded at any time, it can't be used in court. The court must be sure that the item examined in the forensic lab is the same item that was taken from the scene. No-one is allowed to **tamper** with evidence!

Crime scene investigators sometimes wear special overalls to keep their own stray hairs and body bits to themselves.

16

Investigators can spray a special chemical on an area. If there is blood there, it will glow in the dark. Chemicals have also been used to show up this shoe impression in blood.

How to Examine a Crime Scene

1. Protect the scene from onlookers who might destroy evidence.

2. Take detailed notes. Describe everything you see.

3. Take photographs in a clockwise pattern around the scene.

4. Make a rough sketch or diagram of the scene. Add all measurements, such as the width and height of doors, windows and furniture.

5. Carry out a detailed search. Divide the scene into a **grid**. Check each grid for evidence. Don't forget to look up at the ceiling. Evidence can be anywhere!

6. Record all evidence.

Cracking the Case

Back in the crime lab, forensic experts analyse the evidence. Fingerprints can prove that a suspect was at the crime scene. Every person has his or her own set of fingerprints. But they are normally invisible. Sometimes they can be made visible in the lab by passing a small laser over the evidence. Any fingerprints there will glow in the laser beam.

Every cell in your body contains deoxyribonucleic [dee-OX-ee-RYE-bo-new-CLAY-ic] acid. That's DNA for short! We all have different DNA just like we all have different fingerprints. Forensic scientists can analyse DNA from a drop of blood, a tiny piece of skin, saliva or even the root of a pulled-out hair. The result is a picture of a set of bands that looks like a barcode.

FORENSIC TEST ORDER

fingerprints . . . . ☑⇐
DNA . . . . ☑⇐
ballistics . . . . ☐⇐
blood splatter patterns . ☐⇐
hair and fibre . . . . . . ☐⇐
soil and dust . . . . ☐⇐
broken glass . . . . ☐⇐
paint comparison . . . . ☐⇐
shoe and tyre prints . . ☐⇐

Q: Why are potatoes good detectives?
A: They keep their eyes peeled!

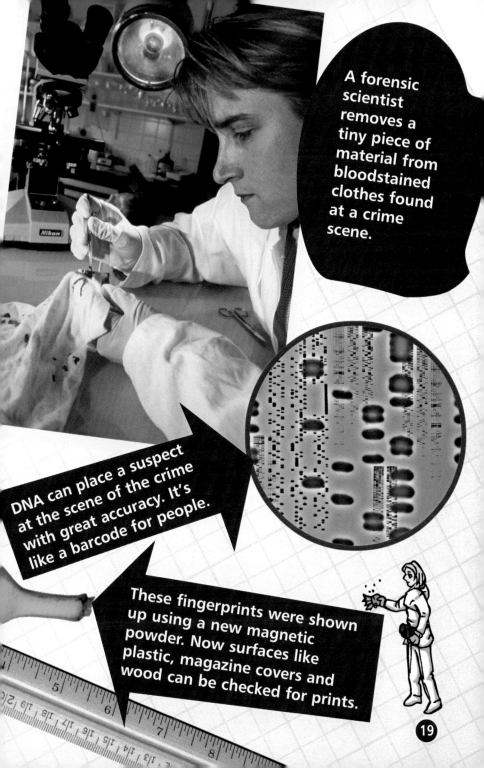

A forensic scientist removes a tiny piece of material from bloodstained clothes found at a crime scene.

DNA can place a suspect at the scene of the crime with great accuracy. It's like a barcode for people.

These fingerprints were shown up using a new magnetic powder. Now surfaces like plastic, magazine covers and wood can be checked for prints.

Murder on Ice

Imagine hiking along a snowy mountain ridge. Suddenly you stumble — and realise you've tripped over a frozen body!

That's just what happened in 1991 to hikers in the Ötzal Alps, near the border of Austria and Italy. They made the grisly find on a lonely mountain 3 200 metres above sea level. The upper part of the body was sticking out of the melting ice. Was it another hiker who had become lost or slipped? Was it a murder victim? Or was it something else?

Who Is the Iceman?

The first investigators to reach the scene found that the body was a male, about 45 years old and with a number of tattoos. The body was well-preserved, so they assumed he had been dead for only a short time.

It then took Alpine Rescue Service four days to reach the site and dig the body from its icy grave. At one stage, a **pneumatic hammer** was used to dig around the body. This damaged the left hip. Finally, the body was wrapped in strong plastic foil and taken by helicopter to a forensic lab in Innsbruck, Austria.

Forensic scientists would determine the cause of death. At this stage, they had not ruled out murder.

Wasn't me!

I didn't do it!

Was this really a modern person? As the body began to thaw, some onlookers noticed that the Iceman was dressed in furs and grass clothes.

Stone Age Mummy

Back in the forensic lab, tests were carried out on the frozen body. Imagine the shock when the Iceman turned out to be not 45 years old, but 5 300 years old! He was, in fact, the oldest and best-preserved natural **mummy** ever found. The forensic team sent for the archaeologists!

Archaeologists are like detectives. They look for clues, too. But they're not looking for clues to a crime; they're looking for clues to the past. The archaeologists called the Iceman 'Ötzi' and set out to investigate his mystery.

Ötzi lived at a time before people could write and record their history. But dead men do tell tales. At least, they tell them to archaeologists who know how to piece the puzzle together.

Ötzi was about 162 cm tall. His body was so well-preserved that his skin and soft tissues were still intact.

Gathering Clues

Scientists didn't want to use any **preservatives** on Ötzi's body. If they did, it could change things in his body and ruin future research. So today his body is kept in conditions just like those in the frozen glacier that he was safely preserved in for thousands of years. He is in a refrigerated glass case in a museum in Italy. About 40 research teams of scientists and archaeologists take turns examining him. But they don't want Ötzi to thaw, so he is only allowed out of cold storage for 11 minutes at a time!

The teams of scientists and archaeologists are slowly piecing Ötzi's story together. The clues are found in his clothes, his tools and even inside his mummified body.

Q: What is an archaeologist?
A: Someone whose career is in ruins

Stomach contents
Wheat bread, green plant, and meat eaten eight hours before Otzi died

26

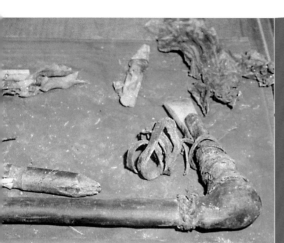

What Happened to the Iceman?

Forgot the snowmobile!

As scientists discover more about Ötzi, they suggest different theories about his death.

Theories
Ötzi died of exhaustion while crossing the Alps.
He froze to death on a hunting trip in rugged terrain.
He fell in a deep **crevasse** in the ice and was quickly covered by a glacier.
He was caught in a snowstorm while bringing his flock back from high pastures.
⇨ Ötzi carried only broken arrows, so he may have had a clash with other humans or wild animals and fled high into the mountains to escape.

Ooops

In 2001, another piece of the jigsaw puzzle was found. X-rays were used to produce a **multi-dimensional** computer image of Ötzi's body. The image showed an arrowhead close to his left lung. He would have died very painfully within a few hours of the wound.

Ötzi was wearing his cloak when he died. It was braided from long grasses, and would have been a waterproof layer over his fur clothes. He probably also used it as a blanket or a ground cover.

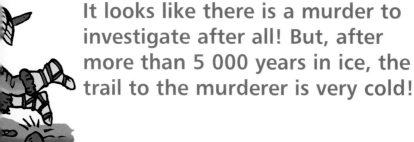

It looks like there is a murder to investigate after all! But, after more than 5 000 years in ice, the trail to the murderer is very cold!

FACT FILE

Legends tell of a rich city called Atlantis that disappeared under the sea about 9 500 BC. Could New Orleans in the United States be the new Atlantis? Some scientists think it will disappear under the sea by the year 2100.

In 1989 it rained sardines on Ipswich, Australia.

My face breaks all the rules!

Scientists have rules to follow to help them reconstruct a face from human remains. The corners of a relaxed mouth are always just behind the canine teeth. Mouths are as wide as the distance between the pupils of the eyes. Eyeballs are 25–26 mm in diameter.

Some flies lay their eggs in dead bodies. Scientists look at how developed the eggs are and try to figure out how long ago they were laid. This gives a clue to when the person may have died!

Some criminals have tried to change their fingerprints with plastic surgery, or by burning or cutting their fingers. But all this does is leave a scar—making the fingerprints easier to identify!

GLOSSARY

crevasse a narrow opening in the ice of a glacier

evidence something that proves a fact

forensic used in a court of law

grid a system of straight lines that cross at right angles

legend a story handed down by tradition

meteors any small bodies travelling through space that enter the Earth's atmosphere

multi-dimensional having more than one dimension, for example depth, width and height

mummy the preserved dead body of a human or animal

pathologists scientists who examine diseases

pneumatic hammer a heavy hammer that works using the pressure of air

preservatives chemicals used to preserve something so that it does not rot

props short for 'propellers'

sterile free from any living germs

suspect a person who is believed to have committed a crime

tamper to damage or change

witnesses people who see a crime

INDEX